ALLES KAPUTT

Santa Fe April 2007

For Gordon + Frances,

A view from the Bottom,

with Good Wishes,

Stanley Noyes

ALLES KAPUTT

POEMS OF WORLD WAR II

◉   ◉   ◉

STANLEY NOYES

TIMBERLINE PRESS
2007

ACKNOWLEDGEMENTS

The author would like to thank the following publications where some of the poems appeared before: *Clark Street Review*, *Blue Unicorn: A Tri-Quarterly of Poetry*, and *Sin Fronteras/Writers Without Borders*. "Last Comanche Code Talker Dies" won a Harold Witt Memorial Award from *Blue Unicorn* (2006).

ISBN 978-0-944048-39-9

Timberline Press
6281 Red Bud
Fulton, Missouri 65251

CONTENTS

"The American Army approaching Germany in the fall of 1944 was in part a Children's Crusade."
—Stephen E. Ambrose, *Citizen Soldiers*

OH, MNEMOSYNE!

You recall outskirts of a city, a plight: a slave
worker, hurt, whom your buddy's driving in a Jeep
to a hospital, and of the trip only this clip survives:
his friend, our guide, on a bike, clinging to the Jeep,
swerves from sunny glass on a dirt road,
and momentarily lets go. Those details
are clear, dirt, pebbles, shards of glass,
as if salvaged from under fathoms, time
as a rich dimension, from its archives, layered
years, a selection of trifling details highlighted.

Yet when Marcel, in the Guermantes' courtyard, trips
on cobblestones, he lives long instants of
bliss, with deep blue coolness, dazzling light,
and finally, possessed by happiness,
recalls irregular paving at St. Mark's
Baptistery in Venice, as he all at once
recovers a perfected instant of his past
enhanced because forgotten for years since—
hence delight, pure appreciation of the actual
that suffuses with value—life. Or is this simply fiction?

Still, remember entering the hospital with two
comrades, and the injured man, greeted
by twin orderlies in white, one of whom
is bald, hair fertile on either side of his dome?
For both parties the struggle to understand
is futile, until you notice peculiar expressions
and inquire about patients glimpsed, *"Ils sont
des fous?"* *"Des aliénés,"* the bald orderly
gently corrects. Yet in the end you leave
the slave, trusting their promise to tend him.

But why, in retrospect, that swerving bike,
patch of dirt seen so clearly, bits
of glass, and not a face, even of your comrade?
The crow swaggering the field pecks some
objects, rejects others. A matter of taste, I guess . . . .
You recollect an anecdote, schema in gray
speech, for pattern and substance. But why, oh
why, does our memory, unlike Marcel's, select
litter, magpies' gatherings of insignificance
without his few precise and haunting images?

Old men resemble mental patients. They forget.
Oh, Mnemosyne, help us old troopers and our wives
recall what matters, mattered long-ago in our lives!

TRAINING, 1944

Moon driving surf, polished waves
succeeding one another, each veined
and marbled peak flattening
in foam, followed by another, thump
and slap and splash, surf crashing
for the beach bearing kelp and froth,
yet recall black night,

                    crawling
            out of Pacific, on knees, hands, shaking,
            babbling, beside comrades, after an hour
            half-submerged, dunked
            again and again, when hissing roller
            after roller surged over the
            heads of men clinging to upset
            craft, until at last boots
            touched, lost, bottom, found
                                sand . . . .

Now . . . sixty years later, jogging wolfdogs,
fortunate oldster, marvel at the moon, moon-
slick ridges, sluicing
froth, veined and marbled surf
folding—still . . . time to
observe quicksilver water's
turbulence, to gaze . . . appreciate.

INTERLUDE, I

Seasoned in rubber boats, salt
surf, till the Bulge.
Crates unpacked. Weapons scoured.

        Le Havre: houses above harbor,
        black window holes.
        Trucks to Camp Lucky Strike.

Waited there almost a lifetime.
Walked nearly once
to village, spire in sky, clouds.

        Open trucks toward front lines
        finally through night countryside.
        Your ticket, a round trip?

RECONNAISSANCE, 1945

Stretched on the beach, face down, gouging
nails in sand, raised my jaw to see,
inches overhead, the brilliant flood
of colored beads that traced a line
from night woods to the Rhine behind us
winding its leisurely course to the North Sea.

We paddled sternforemost back
to our shore, in spite of sergeant L.'s
hanging from that stern, screaming,
"Row for your lives, men!" against a
vibrato from the boscage at our backs,
while Sheehan, by the lieutenant, bled in the bow.

Expectant, I paddled hard, noting,
"I'm still not hit." Approaching our shore
we hollered, *"red knife,"* romantic
watchword, to the shadows there. The sergeant
waded out, vanished in the dark,
never again to be the same man,

and we, we beached the boat. The lieutenant
sped away with Sheehan. We quarreled
about the reconnaissance, spoke, "red knife,"
again, arrived at our billet, kids
still with little to live down—sunrise,
on our lucky Easter Sunday, '45.

CROSSROADS

Captain's orders: spend the night on guard
in your armored car . . . by an intersection.
The lieutenant has picked a handy spot
in which to park . . . the crossroads, holy
site where in Medieval Europe, at times,
any unfortunate hag believed a witch
might be inhumed, stake driven through
her heart. Yet no ghost appears. Merely
a shattering blast and flash.

                            "Move!"
cries the lieutenant. Quickly we shift
from what must have been, I guess,
an X inked in red on the map of some
distant tank commander who'd plotted
coordinates beforehand and zeroed in
his 88, artillery more deadly
than a witch's curse, for a horseshoe
pitch which, luckily for us, missed.

Another day we halt near a shady
knoll, believing a retreating
enemy far, climb down, visit, bunch
to a target, when, abruptly, mortar rounds
whoosh, exploding in our close vicinity. We
hit the dirt, departing later a little
smarter, still lucky, without a casualty.

Nothing prepares you for combat, really:
so this rule—learn and you'll live . . . maybe.

PARTYING WITH PARTISANS
for John Novakovich

That trio of Tito's partisans, their arms
across each other's shoulders, danced
to shrill and rhythmic whistles. Wild
men, they kicked their legs from side
to side in unison, chorus-
line of grim-faced, hardened fighters, while

my buddy, ethnic Serb, and I remained
seated with our hosts behind
our dirty plates and glasses. We banged
the table, bouncing its top in time.
Half-drunk, I was elated: these guys,
freed by other troops, were on our side!

I didn't speak their lingo, nor did they
talk mine. Still their captain offered
me a woman. We two were mute.
I had her once and let her go,
staggered back to the billet, puking,
to end a trooper's perfect evening at war.

FIRING ACROSS THE RHINE

*H*allam opened from the south bank with the 50
caliber on the turret, firing bursts
and the gunner of the M8 on our right with his 50,
both shattering the dark with drumrolls,
streams of color, illuminating a little the water,
and from the far, opposite shore the color
returned with familiar sustained *rips*
of a German gun—but high, and between us,
all those rounds gouging the fields behind.

        Hallam, too, was firing high. "Let me,"
        I asked. He moved aside. Dipping the muzzle,
        gripping the handles, I fired down nearly
        into the ripples, forcing a brilliant streamer,
        formed of white and red arrows, gradually
        across the river to the opposite source of light—
        abruptly extinguished. Mission finished,
        we drove back to our billet in the German village
        where we daily cursed mortar fire from the Rhine.

Had those Krauts run out of ammo? Or
realized they were targets in our crossfire . . . ?
Or had I coolly killed a man? But then
at our last reunion, thirty years beyond the first,
with a mere five troopers and a dozen widows,
the withered wife of a fellow vet, guest
recon, he with far more combat than ours,
stared into my eyes from across the table
and murmured, "Richard came back a different man."

N.B. "recon" in this instance refers to a member of a cavalry
      reconnaissance troop.

We altered less. Did I harden or regress?
Years later I hoped I hadn't killed. That night
it was back to a little boy in short pants
who was, with stolid annoyance, stomping ants.

ONLY BOYS, ONLY MEN

Our convoy, stalled in a German village
by a heap of surrendered weapons, when
a frau comes out from a nearby house to the street
and scolds us, waving her hands:

we know no word of German but perfectly
understand her worry about those guns
and probably the village kids. Instantly then
we become only men and she

just an angry woman, sending us back
to our past, she no longer merely 'an enemy,'
and, though it's none of our business, we
avoid her eyes, fuss with our gear,

sneaking looks at each other, hiding our grins.

POW, 1945

Walking toward the machine gun, the Kraut kid
kept on coming, arms up, till the gunner quit.
They drove him to the tavern we'd commandeered.

He tried to tell us in cryptic English about an aunt . . .
Chicago. But in those woods we'd lost a friend.
My buddies said, "Let's kill him." "Wait," I said,

always having hated the look of blood. "No,
we can't do that." "Why the fuck not?" "Because . . ."
We argued minutes as he stood trying to comprehend,

a little older than a boy, frail, bewildered,
expressionless. A jeep drove up . . . the lieutenant, two
men. The officer jumped out, told them where

to take the prisoner. They drove away.
Sometimes I wonder if he lives and remembers—
an old vet, say, at a Munich beergarden,

raising a tankard to his lips—and thinks of all the springs
since, pictures GI's gripping carbines, arguing,
and realizes how close he came that day, twice, to dying.

GIRL WHO SOLD HER BODY FOR CANDY

A buddy from my platoon ran up panting, "Hey,
corporal, there's this German girl who's putting out
for candy!" Without even thinking, I found
candy and condom, followed directions to building
and room, saw her, plump and frizzy, fully
dressed, a surly girl who seized the payment sulkily.

Action was desperate, clumsy, over with quickly.
I somehow tore her stocking, or panties, and she railed
at me in an alien tongue whose sense was clear. Aside
from momentary delight, the adventure was sordid,
left me in an ugly humor. Departing the hallway
I paused at her jacket dangling, its pockets crammed

with bars of candy. For seconds I tarried and stared,
resisting a nasty temptation to filch her profits
and toss them. For all of a minute I gazed, yet went away
innocent, returned to our billet, laughed, washed up.
and fell into chowline, flushed the scenes from my mind,
forgetting them forever—or so I imagined, at the time.

ALLES KAPUTT

The slaves are going home, trudging
From a Reich in ruins, bombed and burnt up
Cities, heaps of rubble smelling of the dead,
They're tramping all the roads toward home
By burnt-out tanks, by tracks warped and rusted,
Past wrecked freight cars, locomotives-*regardez*,
For instance, that band of Ukranian peasant
Women, thick and short, resembling
Bouncers in headscarves, bright dresses, *en marche*.

      "*Dobra dahn*," or "Good day," I say,
      Mistakenly, to those I imagine Poles,
      "*Bonjour*," to all others in my preppy
      French, hoping they're Belgians or Frenchmen.

I speak français, for instance, to Shorty with scar
For face, wearing beret, who
I learn, is español, labored in a *fabrica*
And understands a bit of what
I say: he's on his way, on foot, back to España.

      Seven years pass. I return, driven,
      To gaze at brick ovens, chimneys
      Within a chainlink fence, a place
      Long ago tidied, not even one
      Whiff of a stench. Yet Suzanne told me
      Of how one night in camp she'd crept
      Pressed an ear to the chamber, and heard
      The horror happening within.

But then in '45, just turned 21
In combat, still an ignorant kid

13

More empathetic with men I was trying to kill
Than with our civilians, I saw the issue of *Yank*,
Its starvling cadavers stacked in cords,
And, paralyzed, glimpsed for the first time
The reason I was there, settled down
To continue contributing my miniscule share
In finishing a war I at last understood.

FISHING

In early spring, with clouds and blue,
we, off duty, reposing a day or two
craved fresh chow, and, spying a pond,
the three of us, two buddies and I,
went fishing. Arrived with our grenades
we surprised a naked man, who'd been bathing,
at its edge, drying in the sun—

      it's the one time I've seen a man
      without an ass: no buttocks.
      He turned, regarded us: hollowed eyes,
      dangling penis, skeleton with skin—

I knew where he'd been, but had no gift
except a pack of cigarettes, precious
then. He thanked me I believe, dressed
and left, fearing from experience, I guess,

      all armed men. Too bad he didn't
      linger. You cannot eat cigarettes.

STAFF SERGEANT MIST

*S*taff Sergeant—our car-commander—Mist
blazoned the face of a Plains Indian chieftain,
war bonnet and all, tattooed in red and blue,
upon his snowball shoulder. Part mystery,
part old lady, Mist was a barracks soldier
charged with wild young men. In the Rhineland,

calling from the turret, he ordered Gatson to halt
before a house where, climbing out,
he went inside, while our squad, seated
in machine-gun Jeep, mortar Jeep, and M8,
waited on the road by a row of trees, and those
who had to pee climbed out and peed.

When the sergeant reappeared, cool
and sanctimonious, toting a musette, we
wondered for a moment about the Frau
standing before us in distress, weeping in her apron
as we drove away. Yet we, young
and indifferent, soon ceased to puzzle or care.

Shortly, when our European war was over
and we slated for the States, before the Pacific
Theatre, our vehicles collected, barracks bags
dispatched to the troopship, news came
M. P.s had searched our sacks, found heirloom silver
in Mist's—a clue at last to his true character.

SWEET SURRENDER

The village was quiet when we reached it.
Nothing stirred on the central street
(no slinking cat or barking dog), so
the lieutenant fired from his M8
a single explosive round which made a hole
in the first building to the west. And abruptly
the little town erupted: from windows
on either side linen fluttered and wagged
and up the road toward us ran
a delegation, the mayor maybe with several
other dressed-up gents to greet us effusively,
with every show of "welcome, Americans!"

And you know, that was the quickest way
I've ever found of making friends.

CLEAN HANDS

On rapid reconnaissance: we encounter a factory.
It's deserted. But the manager emerges
at attention, in a suit, welcomes us in English.
The lieutenant interrogates the chubby boss,
while we check his office, which is simple and neat,
but across from a picture window, a wall
flaunts a flag with swastika black as an SS boot.

Kicking out glass, we exit by the shortest route,
dropping the flag in the dirt by the fellow's foot.
Earnestly he protests his position requires
that banner, but he never has been truly a Nazi,
always admired Roosevelt, American democracy.
Oh, surely. We leave him by his trampled flag, forlornly
important figure, unhappy in his Aryan skin and suit.

"Surely," we chuckle once again, as, departing,
we place more faith in the constancy of clouds
above our 'Cock of the Walk' than in this Nazi's truth.

PARTYTIME

Returning by a village we'd left behind
we chanced upon a celebration, though not
of natives. Infantry to our rear had arrived,
were jigging in the street. One jocose G.I.
dressed in top hat, frock coat, surely borrowed
from a burgher's closet, waved his beermug
as we drove by. Oh, it was a party to surpass
any those villagers had witnessed, no doubt! But
for us a glimpse sufficed. On duty, we sped away,
grimly businesslike, declining the invitation,

if it was that. No, the cavalry's pride
forbids boisterous revelry in the street
so we rode off safe in our knowledge of
the case of booze strapped to the bow of our armored
M8, superior to such juvenile sport.

GAMBLERS

Billeted in two buildings, we troopers shared the first,
lieutenant and rest of our platoon a second
next-door. Back from behind enemy lines,
wound tight as tops, we'd received our ration
of liberated booze. Klem, at the officer's
house, had fabricated a potion he called a 'panzerfaust,'
that German version of our bazooka. We all

drank some. After arguing with the lieutenant
on the topic of racial equality, I returned to our billet,
completely sober, I was certain. Even so . . .
when I entered during a card game, surely poker,
with several spellbound players, several kibitzers,
and no head turned at my entrance, it just seemed,

well, too static, and a scene from boyhood Westerns
flashed, inducing me to draw my personal
sidearm and fire a hole through the ceiling, momentarily
forgetting our beds up there, and perhaps a friend—
but, *action, camera*: the gamblers jumped and shrank,
one tumbling: "Hey, Noyes, what the hell!"'
Winner, I yielded my weapon, levitated to bed, and slept.

BEAUTY IN THE CONQUERED CITY

Crackle of shots in the conquered city
hills. Why not? Who cares?
Guns piled everywhere.
As the French would say, *reglement
de comptes*. Settling of scores. All
those slave laborers freed. We
park for a time, waiting, at ease,

near a rope corral, filled
with men, civilians—Nazis? Though
who says? Guarded by G.I.'s. Next,
a young woman, smartly dressed,
approaches the pen, is waved
away. She looks around, sees us.
Beautiful, she comes to—why me?

Confidently. "Excuse me," she begins,
in correct English. "My father's in there.
Please. I need to talk to him."
Confident yet pleading. "Let's see,"
I say, as I slouch to a G.I. on guard.
"Say, this girl needs to talk
to her father." He stares at her, at me,

finally shrugs, OK. I
retreat, watching a tall man
in gray speak earnestly with beauty,
I, watching her profile, with longing.
"Mount up," snaps the command. We
drive off, I with one last glance
at her back, girl I might glimpse on a sidewalk

in San Francisco, my birth city,
near Union Square, about to enter
a bookstore or Prado Restaurant,
I, dogface of little rank,
here in their desolation, unable
to see her face now, imagine the girl
a pink tulip blooming in a cemetery.

KILROY WAS THERE

Kilroy, a medic, once accompanied, at war's
close, a patrol ordered scouting, and when
they paused in trees, after spying, on a nearby

knoll, standing in an opposite grove, a German
officer leaning into his map with two
soldiers, was abruptly tempted by an opportunity

to possess what dangled on a cord from that officer's neck,
field glasses, a fine pair. "Quick, your carbine,"
he whispered in the corporal's ear. Sighting with care,

he squeezed off a shot. The officer dropped, lay still,
his soldiers fleeing to the woods. Kilroy, of course,
claimed those binoculars, his proud war trophy

for years, until his own cardiac arrest.
Yet doesn't it make you wonder if he ever wondered
whether that enemy, at the end of the war, had left

anyone waiting, make you question whether,
finally, those lenses might not have become for Kilroy
the most expensive object he never paid for?

THE SPRING OF '45

Winter, 1944/45: "*Pvt. Donald Schoo of the 80th
Infantry Division recalled seeing one of his buddies
. . . take a hit from an 88 that blew off his left
hand: He was crying and running around yelling,
'I'm going home! Thank you God, I'm going home!'*"
Citizen Soldiers, *Stephen E. Ambrose*

Abundance of guns that spring, ours
and the surrendered, toys that we, off-duty
big kids, traded, played with,
the familiar and the risky souvenirs,

as when I, in a courtyard, aiming
an empty Mauser at the weathercock
top of a house, fired the weapon
I thought unloaded, had to explain

to the lieutenant, or when one of two pals
plucked out his 45, while his comrade
ducked around a building, and the piece
discharged, chipping the cornerstone,

or another pair wrestled, giggling,
one with submachine gun
dangling, and what we called the 'greasegun'
fired through his buddy's shoulder.

The U.S. and Germany sent their youngsters
to finish our war. How those in foxholes
of mud and bloody snow the winter
before would have envied us the luxury

of our horseplay—or the corpses our European
tour that green and fertile spring!

INTO THE SHADOWS

Firing into the woods, taking rockets in
rebuttal, we're lying on leaves in speckled
shadows within the fringe of a Czech forest
listening to rifles from below the hill:
"Hey," quips someone, "I wonder if you get killed
by our guys, do we get a Purple Heart?"
"Shut up, yuh dumb prick." Chuckles. Now
machine gun fire from below. "That's American
too, thirty caliber. Stupid bastards, shooting
at *us*." After a while, silence. Not even birds.

Mist rushes in, stooping. "OK, men. Let's go."
"What happened?" "Lieutenant got through.
Noyes, get the litter!" I run out to the Jeep.
Silver already has the rear of the stretcher:
I get to go first. The lieutenant leads, zigging
slowly through trees. I follow, Silver behind me,
buddies with carbines spread on either side,
and not a shot yet from the dusky interior,
and next the corpse, lying behind a log,
helmet by his head with the red ditch in it.

Our buddy has gone blue and stiff. We pick
up 'dead weight,' lay him on the litter, slog
and stagger toward outside light. Silver
takes the easiest route, a dim road, perfect
for enfilade from behind, but it's my back,
and stumbling to stay up, I keep expecting
slaps. Yet to my surprise, silence,
and none comes. We stagger into sunlight
alive, sky still blue, sun gold leaf
and grass, with me not even hit, and still alive.

I have to sit for a bit to appreciate the spring
season. In the woods, at last, the birds begin.

THE MESSAGE

The message spewed in dashes, dots
from my radio, and I wrote it as it flew
to words on the pad in my palm
and slapped "roger" and "out" on the key

clamped to my thigh. It was the message
we'd been expecting. I wrote it with glee—
nobody wants to die in the final
weeks of a war, not even the German

regulars, perhaps from the Africa Corps,
who'd stacked their arms in the Rhineland: tan,
blond, tough, they'd looked embarrassed,
amused, at surrendering to kids like us.

But now, platoon on a knoll, we'd
advanced far beyond the infantry
to scout the green-gold Czech
countryside on that 7th of May.

Who wants to die on the last day?
I clambered from the hatch before me, ran
to the lieutenant standing in the turret
of his M8, observing with binoculars

fields and woods before us, handed
up the message. He, reading,
"All offensive action ceased . . ."
met my grin with a nod. Back

in the armored car by Gatson, driver,
friend, I declared, "War's over"

once again. So what's ahead?
I wondered: some time? Possibly . . . a life?

THE SOLITARY REAPER

"The music in my heart I bore
long after it was heard no more."
                                    Wordsworth

The platoon stands in formation under a shiny wind
chasing shadows, men at attention, listening
to some lieutenant while above on the hill
a figure in sky green and yellow swings her scythe
sweeping slowly down her swath. How many
men who've never heard of Wordsworth
hold that distant and unattainable Czech girl
in their minds rather than sounds the wind
tears off?

        And the girl, when she pauses at the end
of a row of grain, leaning upon her scythe, as
her eyes repose a moment upon the compact
force of young men below, also foreign,
remote and unknowable, what does she imagine
standing high in the restless wheat, leaning
upon her scythe before she, solitary reaper,
reels about, sweating, and sweeps her scythe
to level the next row, and the next, of waving grain?

MONUMENTS OF PARIS

Crammed within the bed of an army truck
beneath its canopy, we watched the sodden country
pass and withdraw through rain and mist. Was this
Belgium, we wondered, or France again?

Fields and woods in monotonous hues, rising
fog, sometimes a village, quickly passed,
glimpsed through our open canvas back.
Our vehicles, weapons, Rooskies and SS,

left behind, with our relief and dread, and early
vertigo of victory. So, finally, after days
on the road—suddenly, outskirts of a city,
dim buildings: offices, warehouses, factories.

"Hey guys, this has got to be Paris!" Paris,
that I'd always longed to see, city of history,
women and wine! But we kept rolling through grime
slick streets, industrial blocks,

charcoal prints in a drizzle of light, and continued
to convoy toward the Atlantic, le Havre,
the waiting troopship. "So now we can say we've seen
Paree!" a buddy quipped. "Yeah,

but I'm coming back." "Going to hitch?" "Nope,
row." I swore someday, if I lived, to ogle
the Champs-Elysées, Quai Voltaire and Seine,
the Madeleine—and yes, the Folies Bergères! And I did.

HOMECOMING

On the troopship back, we seemed half black,
half white. We slept and ate separately
but walked the deck together, gathered apart.

There appeared to be no animosity, only
an invisible screen. Entering New York Harbor
with a rosy sun, by the Statue of Liberty,

we beheld Manhattan, while standing at the rail,
and every ship or boat we passed
on our ceremonial way, from tug to ocean liner,

saluted us with—was it a triple blast?
—from pleasure boats to freighters, all
honked a welcome. Our vessel blared back.

The sun shone on the blue chop, its little
froth, while a patiotic flag
snapped from every mast. White and black,

we'd made it back alive, were honored as one
for a moment, before dispersing on furlough.
Meanwhile every vessel saluted us

as heroes. Although the Statue blushed
as we passed, a sundry fleet welcomed home
black and white alike, and for a time

we were proud, projecting beyond family
celebrations, beyond even likely
Pacific battles to come, to begin our

fantasies of destinies other than our beginnings
(the choices different, of course, for each color,
each man). Still there was the luster of

hope for many in our vision of Manhattan, billows,
banners, in every vessel's blast, for a history
surpassing the history of our divided past.

TROPHIES

On an eastbound train to rejoin my troop,
and hoping to pick up a girl en route,
I surreptitiously observed
two marines who'd succeeded.

      At 21, I was a man.
      They were boys to me, although
      their ribbons suggested more. Two
      pretty girls absorbed Pacific

yarns with awe. Envious, I watched
the West flash by, until a cry
made me stare: the girls were shocked,
fascinated by the Mason Jar

      one marine, bold and proud
      it seemed, held out. What? Gold . . .
      gleaming? and teeth . . . ? gold-filled?
      Two girls gazed aghast, deliciously thrilled.

TWO TRAINS

Two trains halted in a station, one
eastbound, ours headed west, stopped for minutes,

packed with men. We from the Rhineland and Czech
farmlands, destined for Pacific islands, probably

a beachhead on Japan, leaving friends
behind in Norman fields with rows of crosses.

GI's on the opposite train lean from windows,
men with bandaged arms or heads, as

strolling, we glance through dirty glass to see,
dim figures within, pallor of gauze or sheets.

Abruptly mocking voices as those casualties,
mistaking us perhaps for green recruits,

replacements, taunt, "You'll be sorry. You'll
be sorry!" over and again. We gaze at their gauze,

silently climb in our cars, wondering why,
even if wounded, men can be so mean,

yet guessing we might have done the same: They,
like us, were merely human, human merely.

CELEBRATING VJ NIGHT IN CHICAGO

Stepped off a train in Chicago to headline heaven:
JAPAN SURRENDERS, this buddy and I. Still numb
to its meaning for us, we were hungry to party.

Roaming the streets, we paused at buildings
where women leaned from second-floor windows
cheering and waving. We waved lustily back,

hoping maybe to lure a knowing pair
of passionate dates for the evening. Upstairs,
we found all feminine heads bent to their work:

not one looked up. But later prowling neon
blocks, we seized two eager older teens
out of the rollicking crowd, bought them drinks,

courted them, believed we were making time:
we, their very own soldiers! They invited us home . . .
to meet their folks! *Whoa!* With gentle persistence

we broke their grips on our palms, to close
the night behind a sign: Manhattan with winking
cherry and crimson letters spelling BAR—

no longer B for Browning, A for Auto-
matic, R for Rifle—simply this tavern
in which, glum, we had at last to grin

and chuckle at how hard those girls had clung,
unaware of wrecking our plans for the evening.
In the end we toasted VJ night with a laugh.

INTERLUDE II, PEACE 1945

Swore, with luck, to come back:
L'Ile de France. Le Midi.
Never reached that spire, Combray.

      Fell in love with white and blue
      Mediterranean, its buildings,
      lavender, pink, piled above.

What luck to survive! Fields
of red poppies, crosses—
criminal not to prize your life.

      Fell in love with language of Proust,
      his France, steeples, hawthorns.
      row of trees on the road to Balbec.

STRANGERS TO THIS SHORE

Early morning beach walk, and low tide,
and so this expanse of wet sand, with noisy surf
withdrawing in spite of an onshore breeze
wagging grass on dunes. Striding fast,
breathe deeply, glad of clouds in a vast,

tinted sky—until this question: what's above
the foamline, surely abandoned by the tide, some
brown and pink shapelessness? Pass
a boot as I stop to stare. Yes, the pink's
a bloated belly and chest in brown pants.

The thing sprawled, mannequin once a man, possesses
a face like a bald head twisted toward land, sanded,
with no feature except for nose smashed perhaps
by rocks, the whole a blank, pink, streaked red.
You think—repugnance, fear? Well, it's grim,

but there's no stink yet, merely fresh breeze
off the Pacific. Walking back fast recall
their bringing Conklin's body in, stowing it
in a room by the door of that inn we took over
and how the stench insinuated everywhere.

I think of that friend's cadaver and of this
reminder after nearly 60 years after
that ancient war, I think, breathing deeply
sea air, of my oldest enemy and friend, still there
within, and of that poor bastard, stranger here

like many, of choices, uncertainties, certainties
and think, no matter how we end, death's no spook:
merely absence of life in what was alive, like them.

LAST COMANCHE CODE TALKER DIES
AP.

For the Comanche code talkers
and all W.W. II Vets, Dead and Alive

After Roderick Red Elk dies the Stars
and Stripes sag at half-mast, and the Nuhmuhnuh
honor his memory and Charles Chibitty, now last
of fourteen to land on Utah Beach, D-Day, '44,
who fought the entire war to Hitler's Reich:
the drummers and singers praise them all, G.I.s
of my nation, though I not one of theirs
as I was reminded . . . Comanche Nation Fair
'97 . . . by singers, colors, dancers, drummers.

After the Scalp Dance, victory rite rendered
by women, Comanche vets and younger men
trail Chibitty, shuffling a long circle
around the arena. To honor a warrior, offer a few
bucks and a handshake. Because it was my war,
too, a lifetime ago, this old vet walks out, offers his gift
and shakes that hard hand. "I was there," I say,
"Spring of '45." Chibitty's gaze never wavers. Back
with spectators, I reflect, "A distant comrade,

in time and place," and years after gripping the hand,
of the codetalker, I still know who honored whom.

FOREST ROAD AT NIGHT

for Keith & Heloise Wilson

The moon projects naked aspen shadows
across the snowy road, skeletons,
while still alive. Pale trees
form iron bars to stride upon
and through. An imaginary prison opens
progressively under a lunar glow.

I gaze into the woods and note
a multitude of trees descending
down the canyon to the creek. They rise
stark from snow, stained with shadows.
"If trees were men?" I muse . . . Yes, my troop,
my division, a few old men and the dead.

◎   ◎   ◎

This edition of *Alles Kaputt: Poems of World War II*
by Stanley Noyes
was handset in 12 pt. Garamond Old Style
with Modern Gothic display
and hand-printed on a 6x10 C&P.

Text paper is Wausau Royal Linen, and the cover is
Neenah Classic Linen with Wausau Royal Silk
end-paper.

All design, printing, and
hand-binding were by
Clarence Wolfshohl
at
Timberline Press
2006-2007

◎   ◎

◎